Breakthrough Inventions

INVENTING THE CAMERA

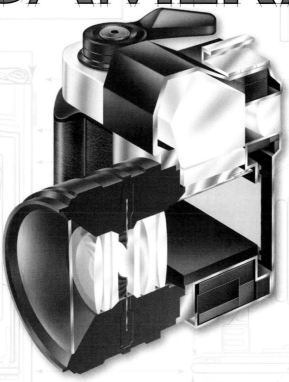

Joanne Richter

 Crabtree Publishing Company

www.crabtreebooks.com

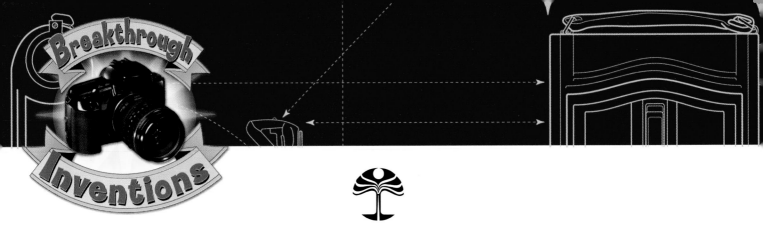

Crabtree Publishing Company

www.crabtreebooks.com

Coordinating editor: Ellen Rodger

Series and project editor: Adrianna Morganelli

Designer and production coordinator: Rosie Gowsell

Production assistant: Samara Parent

Scanning technician: Arlene Arch-Wilson

Art director: Rob MacGregor

Project development, editing, photo editing, and layout: First Folio Resource Group, Inc.: Tom Dart, Greg Duhaney, Sarah Gleadow, Debbie Smith

Photo research: Maria DeCambra

Consultants: Todd Gustavson, Technology Curator, George Eastman House; Colin Harding, Curator of Photographic Technology at the National Museum of Photography, Film and Television, Bradford, United Kingdom; Shannon Thomas Perich, Associate Curator, Photographic History Collection, Smithsonian's National Museum of American History

Photographs: Ansel Adams Publishing Rights Trust/Corbis: p. 27; AP Wide World Photo: p. 18 (top), p. 25 (bottom); Art Archive/National Archives Washington D.C.: p. 13; Colin Bentley: p. 20 (both), p. 21 (top, both); Bettmann/Corbis: p. 9 (bottom), p. 14 (top); Canada Science and Technology Museum: p. 11 (top); Corbis: p. 12 (bottom); Leonard de Selva/Corbis: p. 8 (top); George Eastman House: p. 10 (top), p. 17 (both), p. 18 (bottom); Giraudon/Art Resource, NY: p. 7 (top); Granger Collection, New York: p. 15 (top); Barbara Henry/istock International: p. 15 (bottom); Dora Horton: p. 8 (bottom); Hulton-Deutsch Collection/Corbis: p. 12 (top); icenine photography/istock International: pp. 16-19 (timeline); David Lees/Corbis: p. 5 (bottom); Erich Lessing/Art Resource, NY: p. 4; Rob MacGregor: p. 19 (bottom), p. 24 (bottom), p. 30 (bottom), p. 31 (bottom); Kimmo Mjntyll/Rex Features/CP: p. 30 (top); Allison Napier: p. 21 (bottom, both); National Museum of Photography, Film & Television/Science & Society Picture Library: p. 16; Joseph Nicéphore Niépce/Gernsheim Collection, University of Texas, Austin, USA, Archives Charmet/Bridgeman Art Library: p. 7 (bottom); NMPFT/Science & Society Picture Library: p. 10 (bottom), p. 14 (bottom); Oxford Science Archive/Heritage-Images/The Image Works: p. 5 (top); Janice Carr/Public Health Image Library (7815), Public Health Image Library (3362): p. 28 (both); Science Museum/Science & Society Picture Library: p. 6 (top), p. 11 (bottom); p. 19 (top); William Henry Fox Talbot/NMPFT/SSPL/The Image Works: p. 9 (top); Image by courtesy of the Wedgwood Museum Trust, Staffordshire (England): p. 6 (bottom); Vaughn Youtz/Zuma/Corbis: p. 31 (top); Other images from stock CD.

Illustrations: www.mikecarterstudio.com: title page, pp. 22–23

Cover: While early cameras often required professional skills to operate, many cameras today are simple in design and can be used by anyone, including kids.

Title page: With a manual single-lens reflex (SLR) camera, a photographer turns dials and presses buttons to adjust the picture that the camera captures.

Contents: Many cameras still use 35mm camera film today.

Crabtree Publishing Company

www.crabtreebooks.com   1-800-387-7650

Cataloging-in-Publication Data
Richter, Joanne.
    Inventing the camera / Joanne Richter.
    p. cm. -- (Breakthrough inventions)
    Includes bibliographical references and index.
    ISBN-13: 978-0-7787-2814-6 (rlb)
    ISBN-10: 0-7787-2814-5 (rlb)
    ISBN-13: 978-0-7787-2836-8 (pbk)
    ISBN-10: 0-7787-2836-6 (pbk)
    1. Cameras--History--Juvenile literature. I. Title. II. Series.
TR250.R43 2006
770--dc22
                                        2005035441
                                        LC

Published in the United States
PMB 16A
350 Fifth Ave.
Suite 3308
New York, NY
10118

Published in Canada
616 Welland Ave.
St. Catharines
Ontario, Canada
L2M 5V6

Published in the United Kingdom
White Cross Mills
High Town, Lancaster
LA1 4XS
United Kingdom

Published in Australia
386 Mt. Alexander Rd.
Ascot Vale (Melbourne)
VIC 3032

Contents

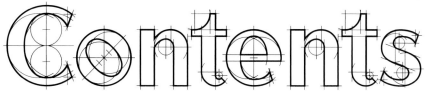

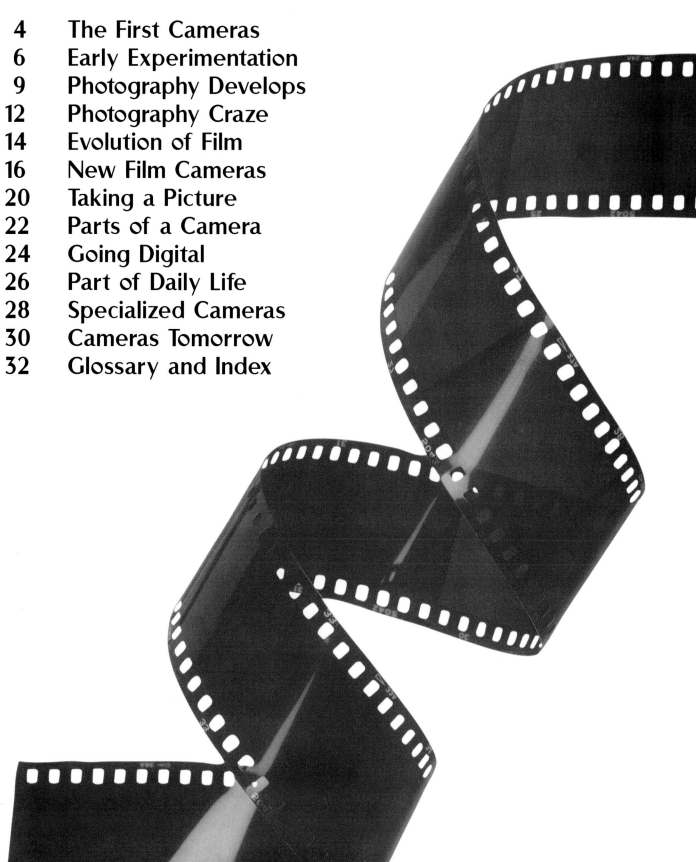

The First Cameras

For millions of people around the world, using a camera is the perfect way to capture a special moment. For others, it is an essential tool for business, learning, and creating works of art.

What is a Camera?

A camera, whether film or digital, is simply a sealed dark box. A lens at the front allows light to enter, and light-sensitive material inside records an image. The modern camera developed from an earlier invention, the camera obscura, which formed an image by directing rays of light through a tiny hole.

Before the camera was invented, artists drew or painted what they saw. This required long training and expensive materials, and was very time consuming. The invention of photography allowed people to create images in an instant.

Light Through a Pinhole

As early as the 400s B.C., **philosophers**, such as Mo-tzu from China, observed that when light bouncing off an object traveled through a pinhole and hit a surface on the other side, it produced an upside-down and backward image of the object. Around 1000 A.D., an Arabian **scholar** named Al-Hazen wrote about the effects of light shining through a pinhole into a darkened room. This was the first accurate description of what would later be named a camera obscura, which means "dark room" in **Latin**. Al-Hazen and many other scientists used the camera obscura to study the behavior of light.

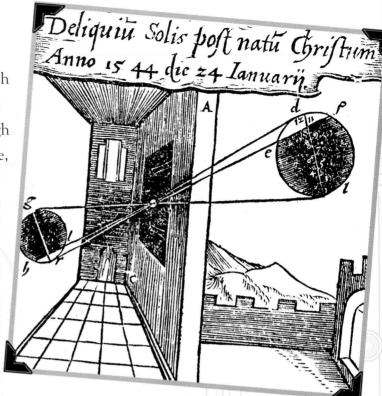

(above) Astronomers *used camera obscuras to watch* solar eclipses *so they would not damage their eyes by looking directly at the sun. Sunlight passing through the hole created a tiny picture of the sun on the opposite wall.*

The Changing Camera Obscura

In the 1500s, the camera obscura changed as artists began to use it as a drawing aid. A glass lens replaced the hole to help focus the light and brighten the image. Inside the room, a mirror was sometimes positioned behind the lens and angled to reflect an upright image for viewing or tracing onto paper. By the 1600s, the darkened rooms were replaced by portable tents or wooden huts, and, soon after, by simple tabletop box models, which were smaller and easier to move from place to place.

(left) A mirror inside this early box camera obscura reflected images onto tracing paper. The paper was placed on a glass shelf beneath the camera's hood. Using this camera, people with no art training could trace and color a picture, and achieve lifelike results.

Early Experimentation

Images produced by the camera obscura were not lasting ones. As soon as the light disappeared, so did the images. From the 1600s to the 1800s, many inventors tried to make permanent images with camera obscuras, using chemical mixtures that darkened when they were exposed to light.

Thomas Wedgwood

In 1802, Thomas Wedgwood, of England, brushed a sheet of paper with a **solution** of silver nitrate, placed a scene painted on glass on the paper, and exposed it to sunlight. After several hours, a negative image appeared on the paper. A negative reverses light and dark in an image. The light areas of the painting appeared dark and the dark areas appeared light. Wedgwood could only view the images by candlelight because the paper continued to react in the daylight until it was completely black.

Joseph Nicéphore Niépce

In 1816, Joseph Nicéphore Niépce, from France, used Wedgwood's ideas to try to print real-life scenes captured by the camera obscura. He prepared paper the same way Wedgwood had, and placed it inside a small box camera so it would be exposed to light. Niépce was able to capture negative images, but they soon blackened, like Wedgwood's pictures.

(left) Thomas Wedgwood failed to make permanent images from real life with a camera obscura. Most likely, the chemicals he used were not strong enough to fix the image to a surface.

(above) In 1778, English inventor William Storer designed a camera with three lenses that could capture an image in candlelight, as well as in daylight.

The Birth of Photography

Niépce then turned to printing metal plates, hoping to create lasting, positive images. In 1827, he coated a small plate with a sticky material called bitumen of Judea, which was used to pave roads. He placed the plate in the back of a camera obscura, positioned the camera obscura in front of a third-story window in his home, and uncapped the lens to let sunlight shine in. After eight hours, the view from the window appeared on the plate. The brightest parts of the scene lightened and hardened the bitumen. Niépce dissolved the parts of the bitumen that the sun had not hardened, which revealed the metal plate underneath. The result was a permanent, positive image, and the world's first photograph. Niépce called his invention "heliography," from the Latin words for "sun drawing."

Joseph Nicéphore Niépce took the world's first photograph with a very basic camera that he built himself.

Louis Jacques Mandé Daguerre

Louis Jacques Mandé Daguerre was a French painter who created enormous, lifelike pictures that audiences viewed in theaters as lights shone on them. He created the scenes by projecting images from a camera obscura onto paper, and then tracing and painting the scenes by hand. Like many artists of his time, Daguerre wished that the camera could make its own permanent images, and he began to experiment in 1824.

This view from Niépce's home is the world's first photograph. Niépce could only take pictures of motionless objects because the exposure time for heliographs was very long.

Daguerreotypes

In 1835, Daguerre discovered a way to permanently capture images that reduced **exposure times** from several hours to less than half an hour. Daguerre tried to capture an image with a camera obscura when the sky became cloudy. There was not enough light to continue, so he put the copper plate he was using in a drawer and forgot about it.

Later, Daguerre removed the plate to find that an image had appeared on it. He had accidentally discovered the idea of the latent, or hidden, image. Plates coated with silver, which reacts to light, held an "invisible" image after a short exposure time. A chemical made the image appear. In Daguerre's case, the chemical was from a broken thermometer in the drawer. His photographs, called daguerreotypes, were sharp, but their silver surface could only be seen from certain angles.

In 1829, Louis Daguerre and Nicéphore Niépce agreed to work as partners. After Niépce died in 1833, Daguerre continued to improve on Niépce's photographic techniques.

With the shortened exposure time needed for daguerreotypes, photographers could take pictures of people, since they were not required to sit still for as long as with earlier cameras. Daguerreotypes were often mounted under glass in fancy frames and cases to keep them from tarnishing.

Photography Develops

Once word of the daguerreotype spread, artists and scientists around the world began to share their developments in photography. The word "photography" was first used by the English scientist Sir John Herschel, at a lecture in 1839. The term comes from the Greek words for "writing with light."

William Henry Fox Talbot

In 1835, William Henry Fox Talbot, from England, developed the calotype process. This process, named from the Greek word for "beautiful," created negative photographs that were not very sharp, but that could be used to make unlimited copies of positive prints.

The first photograph that William Henry Fox Talbot took using the calotype process was of a window in his home. Talbot received a patent for the process in 1841.

The Calotype

With a camera obscura, Talbot captured a permanent negative image on paper treated with salt and silver nitrate. He exposed the paper for 30 seconds, developed it with chemicals, and a negative image appeared. To make a positive print, or one that showed light as light and dark as dark, Talbot coated the negative in oil or wax until it was **transparent**. He laid it on top of another sheet of light-sensitive paper. As sunlight shone on the transparent negative, the darkened areas kept the print from turning dark, while the light areas allowed the light through. By repeating the process, Talbot made many copies of the same positive print. Making positive prints from negatives is a basic process still used today.

William Henry Fox Talbot's photograph The Ladder *appeared in* The Pencil of Nature*, one of the first books to be illustrated with photographs.*

The Collodion Revolution

The next challenge for inventors was to produce images that were as sharp as daguerreotypes, and could be reproduced, or copied, on paper, like calotypes. In 1851, Frederick Scott Archer of England, invented the wet-collodion process. Archer applied a thick, clear solution called collodion to a glass plate, then bathed the plate in light-sensitive silver nitrate. He placed the plate inside a camera and exposed it for a few seconds. After the plate was bathed in developing chemicals, a crisp, sharp negative image appeared. Archer used the plate to make many copies of positive prints.

This camera, built around 1860, was designed to hold wet-collodion glass plates. The camera's lens, mounted in brass, was designed for taking portraits.

Short Exposure Times

Archer's glass plates were so sensitive to light that exposure times became very short — only a few seconds. Objects in motion, such as clouds, water, or people walking, could be captured in photographs for the first time.

The problem with wet-collodion photography was that the plates had to be prepared, exposed, and developed while the collodion was still wet. Photographers could only work in studios, with their supplies nearby, or they had to travel with their chemicals and their large portable **darkrooms**.

The wet-plate process required careful mixing of many different chemicals. Photographers did this, as well as prepared glass plates, themselves.

Chloride of Gold. For the. Toning. Bath

Crystal Varnish.
Institution, 168, New Bond

No 7.

The Dry-Plate Process

The invention of a new process in the 1870s made photography much simpler. Richard Leach Maddox, from England, wrote about coating glass plates with light-sensitive silver compounds and gelatin, a clear, thick liquid obtained from animals. Unlike glass plates coated with collodion, gelatin plates did not have to be used while wet. Photographers could store prepared plates in the dark for later use. In 1878, Charles Bennett, also from England, perfected the first fast dry plates, and by the middle of the 1880s, the dry-plate process had largely replaced the wet-plate one.

Richard Leach Maddox published his idea of coating glass plates with gelatin in the British Journal of Photography *in 1871.*

To take photographs, dry plates were placed in holders such as these, loaded into cameras, and uncovered before opening the lens. After exposure, the plates were re-covered and removed from the cameras for processing.

Shutters

The exposure times needed for the new plates were so short that shutters were added to the fronts of lenses to control the amount of light entering cameras. The earliest shutters were wooden boards or metal sheets, each with a small hole. Photographers let the shutters drop for just long enough to expose the dry plates to light. Viewfinders, which are windows attached to cameras above the lenses, were also added so photographers could see what they were photographing as they took pictures.

Smaller Cameras

When exposure times were long, photographers placed their cameras on stands or tables to keep them steady. If they held the cameras themselves, they shook, which caused the images to be blurry. With shorter exposure times, photographers were able to hold the cameras in their hands, and cameras became smaller and more portable.

Photography Craze

For most of the 1800s, the general public did not own cameras because they were unable to afford them, and developing images required skill. People enjoyed looking at photographs and had professional photographers take their pictures.

Posing for Portraits

When the daguerreotype was introduced in 1839, excited customers flocked to portrait studios to have their photographs taken. Even people with little money to spare made annual trips to the studios, dressed in their finest clothes. Posing for a photograph was not easy. Sitters had to sit still for up to two minutes in intense sunlight without blinking. Cameras needed long exposure times or the image would be blurry. This is why the people in old photos look stiff and did not smile. As techniques and equipment improved, exposure times grew shorter. This brought in a new age of lightning-speed photography. Suddenly, people could capture images of bustling streets, action on sports fields, and animals in motion.

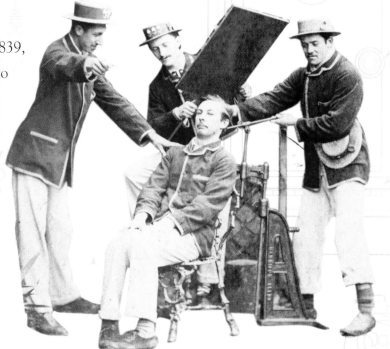

(above) A vise sometimes held the sitter's head and neck still while a photographer measured the amount of available light and took a picture.

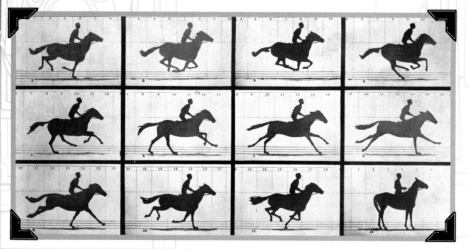

(left) In 1878, Eadweard Muybridge set up 12 cameras in a row to capture a series of photographs of a galloping horse. His photos were solid proof that all four of a horse's legs left the ground in mid-gallop.

12

Pioneers Behind the Lens

Photographs were a powerful way for the public to learn about unfamiliar people, places, and events. In the 1860s, Matthew Brady left his successful portrait studio to take photographs of **American Civil War** battlefields. He and a team of more than 20 photographers took pictures of the wounded and dead. The images gave the public a close-up look at the horrors of war for the first time in history. Other early photographers took pictures of the American West and of people and land in other countries.

New Industries

Many new industries developed as photography became more popular. More books were published with photographs rather than with illustrations, and many books about photography became available. Factories that made photography equipment and stores that sold equipment opened everywhere. Museums, galleries, and fairs began holding competitions for the best photographs. A new age of image reproduction had begun.

Matthew Brady's stark photographs showed the devastating results of the American Civil War.

Evolution of Film

Early photography meant using awkward glass plates, dangerous chemicals, and complicated steps to produce an image. The invention of film changed photography forever by making it simpler and popular with the general public.

George Eastman

George Eastman was a bank clerk from Rochester, New York, whose photography hobby led him to invent new ways of making photographs. Eastman's hobby turned into a job when he began making photographic film, and later, cameras. In 1884, he patented his invention of paper roll film to replace glass plates. Paper roll film was a strip of paper coated with a light-sensitive gelatin film, rolled on a spool, and sealed inside a wooden case. It allowed photographers to take 24 pictures without having to load and unload fragile plates. After each exposure, the key wound the film forward to a new **frame**. Eastman set up a company to make and sell his film.

(above) George Eastman took photographs of himself to test his new film in 1884.

(left) With Eastman's paper film, the grain of the paper often showed up in photographs, making them less clear. In 1887, Reverend Hannibal Goodwin, from New Jersey, invented the first *flexible*, transparent film, and Eastman began to manufacture it two years later.

Kodachrome

George Eastman's company, called Eastman Kodak, introduced the first color film, called Kodachrome in 1936. Kodachrome film included three layers of silver compounds, each one sensitive to a different color: red, green, or blue. The colors of pictures taken with Kodachrome film were true to life, and the images were brilliant and sharp.

Color Your World

Eastman created black and white film. The first color images were hand tinted, or painted black and white images. One of the first successful types of color photography was called Autochrome, which was patented in 1903 by Auguste and Louis Lumière of France. The Lumière brothers coated glass plates with layers of silver compounds, gelatin, and grains of potato **starch** that were dyed blue, green, and red. The dyed starch filtered light, or allowed different colors of light to get through to the light-sensitive silver compounds. Blue light could travel through blue potato starch, green light through green potato starch, and red light through red potato starch.

(above) An Autochrome photograph appeared colored when viewed under light.

35 mm Film

Before the 1930s, film came in many different sizes, and resulted in prints that were the same size as the negatives. The use of 35 mm film became popular in the 1930s. It produced negatives that could be enlarged to make larger prints without losing any sharpness.

High-quality 35 mm film was first used for moviemaking.

New Film Cameras

The first camera sold to the public was a daguerreotype camera made in France by Alphonse Giroux. Introduced in 1839, it was a simple plate camera based closely on the camera obscura. The camera has changed and improved since then, especially since the introduction of film.

Panoramic Cameras

Photographs depicting panoramic, or wide, views have been popular since the earliest days of picture taking. At first, photographers took a series of side-by-side images, and then lined them up and displayed them together. In 1843, Friedrich von Martens built and used the first rotating camera that could take a panoramic photograph on a single, curved glass plate. German manufacturer Rudolph Stirn introduced the Wonder Panoramic Camera, the first panoramic camera using roll film, in 1890.

The Kodak

In 1888, George Eastman introduced the first handheld camera designed for flexible film, called the Kodak. The Kodak came loaded with film for 100 photographs. Users sent their cameras to Eastman's factory, where their photographs were developed. The company returned the pictures and the cameras, reloaded with new film, to the customers. The slogan for the Kodak was, "You press the button — we do the rest."

(above) During the mid-1800s, panoramic photographs were displayed for the public.

1839	**1843**	**1861**	**1884**	**1887**
The Giroux Daguerreotype is the first camera sold.	The first panoramic camera takes extra-wide photographs.	The first single-lens reflex camera is patented.	George Eastman introduces paper roll film.	Reverend Hannibal Goodwin invents the first flexible, transparent film.

More than 100,000 Brownies were sold in their first year of production.

Single-Lens Reflex Cameras

The single-lens reflex, or SLR camera is a type of camera that became popular in the mid-1900s. In SLR cameras, a mirror is placed between the lens and the film. The mirror reflects the image seen through the lens into a viewfinder. Then, the mirror sweeps out of the way just before the picture is taken. The first SLR camera was patented in 1861 by Thomas Sutton. The German company Ihagee introduced the first single-lens reflex 35 mm camera, the Kine Exakta, in 1936.

The Brownie

The Kodak camera was successful, but it was expensive. It cost $25, a large amount at the time. Many people could not afford to buy a camera until 1900, when the Eastman Kodak Company introduced the Brownie camera. Brownies were made of wood and cardboard, and cost only $1, less than a day's wages.

35 mm Cameras

In 1913, Paul Dietz, an Austrian living in the United States, applied for a patent for the Tourist Multiple, the first camera designed to hold 35 mm film. That same year, the Leitz company, based in Germany, built a **prototype** of the 35 mm camera designed by their inventor, Oskar Barnack. The outbreak of **World War I** put the development of 35 mm cameras on hold. Only about 1,000 Tourist Multiples were ever built, and Leitz's camera, the Leica I, was not introduced to the public until 1925.

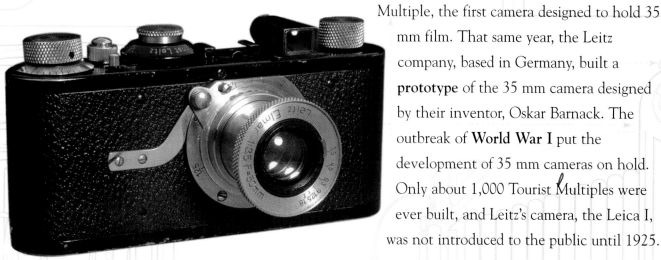

The compact, fast, and reliable Leica I, whose name combined "Leitz" and "camera," became popular with professional photographers and camera enthusiasts around the world.

1888	**1900**	**1903**	**1913**	**1925**
George Eastman launches the Kodak camera.	Kodak introduces the Brownie camera.	The Lumière brothers patent Autochrome color film.	The Tourist Multiple is the first 35 mm camera sold.	The Leica I, the first successful 35 mm camera, is launched.

Automatic Exposure Control

Before automatic exposure control was invented, photographers had to estimate how much light was available when and where they were taking pictures. Then, they set their cameras' lens openings, or apertures, **manually** to let in the right amount of light. The folding Super Kodak Six-20 camera of 1938 was the first camera with automatic exposure control. This camera sensed the brightness of the available light, and automatically adjusted the settings to let in just the right amount.

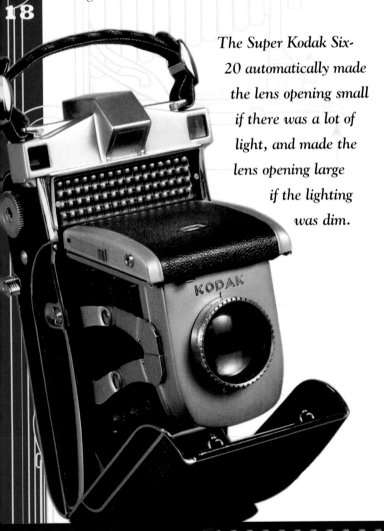

The Super Kodak Six-20 automatically made the lens opening small if there was a lot of light, and made the lens opening large if the lighting was dim.

Instant Cameras

Instant cameras differed from ordinary film cameras because they developed their own film. The first instant camera, the Model 95 Polaroid Land, was launched in 1948. It allowed users to take, develop, and print a black-and-white photograph in about 60 seconds.

The camera contained negative paper, print paper, and developing chemicals. When a picture was taken, the negative and print papers were sandwiched together, with the chemicals in between. Then, the user pulled the sheet out of the camera and, after about a minute, peeled the final print away from the negative.

(above) Edwin Land, shown here with a Polaroid picture of himself, invented the first instant camera after his young daughter begged him to show her a photograph right after it was taken.

1936	1938	1948	1960	1976
Ihagee releases the first SLR 35 mm camera; Eastman Kodak introduces Kodachrome film.	The first camera with automatic exposure control is launched.	Edwin Land's Polaroid camera is first sold to the public.	The Calypso, the first underwater camera, is sold to the public.	The first camera run completely by a microcomputer is sold.

Automatic Focus

Before 1977, photographers had to adjust the focus of their cameras by hand. They turned a ring on the cameras until the images in the viewfinders were sharp. The Japanese company Konica sold the first camera with built-in autofocus. The Konica C35 AF automatically focused the lens, allowing photographers to take pictures without adjusting the focus themselves.

Single-Use Cameras

Single-use cameras date back to the 1890s, but the Japanese camera company Fuji reintroduced them in 1986. These simple, inexpensive cameras come preloaded with film. Once the film is finished, the user brings the camera to a photo-processing lab, which develops the pictures and returns the camera body to the manufacturer for recycling.

Electronic Cameras

By 1976, cameras began to be made with electronic features as well as mechanical ones. The Japanese-made Canon AE-1 camera was the first to use a built-in microcomputer instead of moving parts. This reduced the number of parts that needed to be manufactured, as well as the camera's cost.

(above) Behind the front of this 1978 Canon AE-1 is a complex arrangement of circuits.

(right) Single-use film cameras reached the height of their popularity in 2004. Today, single-use digital cameras are being sold.

1977	1986	1990	1994	2005
Autofocus makes its debut.	Fuji reintroduces single-use cameras.	The first digital camera is launched.	Apple Computer releases color digital cameras.	The first digital camera designed for wireless transfers, the Nikon P1, is introduced.

Taking a Picture

When a photograph is taken, light reflected from an object enters a camera through a lens. The light records an image on film, which can be seen when the film is developed.

Focus on Lenses

The lens is the eye of the camera. Today, a camera's lens is actually a series of lenses, which are clear, curved pieces of glass or plastic. The lens directs the light entering the camera onto the film to form an image. Different types of lenses allow photographers to achieve different effects. Telephoto lenses make objects that are far away appear larger. Wide-angle lenses capture more of the width of a scene than regular lenses, and are useful for taking pictures of large groups or scenery.

The photograph to the right was taken with a regular lens, while the photograph below was taken from the same spot with a wide-angle lens.

Setting the Aperture

The aperture is an adjustable opening inside the camera lens that helps control the amount of light entering the camera during an exposure. In very bright light, a small aperture limits the amount of light striking the film so that the picture does not become overexposed, or very light overall. In darker conditions, a large aperture lets in more light so that the picture is not underexposed, or very dark overall.

The aperture size also affects a photograph's depth of field, or how much of a picture is in sharp focus. As the aperture is made smaller, the depth of field gets bigger, meaning that more of the picture is in sharp focus.

(above) In the photograph on the left, a large depth of field means that both the salt and pepper shakers appear reasonably crisp. In the photograph on the right, a shallow depth of field means that only the nearest object — the top of the salt shaker — is in sharp focus.

Open and Shut

Shutter speed is another factor that affects the amount of light entering a camera. A fast shutter speed means that the shutter opens and closes very quickly, letting in little light. Fast shutter speeds allow photographers to capture clear images of moving objects. A slow shutter speed means that the shutter stays open for longer, and lets in more light. Slower shutter speeds allow photographers to take pictures in darker conditions.

(left) The falling leaves of the photograph on the top appear to stand still, thanks to a fast shutter speed. The slow shutter speed of the image on the bottom gives the leaves a blurred appearance.

Parts of a Camera

For decades, serious photographers have used 35 mm SLR cameras. Some models are completely manual, and others have automatic features. Still others offer both automatic features, for convenience, and manual operation, for times when photographers want to control focusing, shutter speed, and aperture settings.

1. Lens: Professional cameras have exchangeable lenses that allow photographers to achieve different effects.

2. Focusing ring: Turning the focusing ring adjusts the camera's focus by moving the lens closer to or farther away from the film.

3. Aperture ring: Turning the aperture ring adjusts the size of the aperture.

4. Mirror: An angled mirror behind the lens reflects the view so that it can be seen through the viewfinder window.

5. Camera body: The body holds all the parts of a camera, and completely keeps out light except during exposures.

6. Shutter release: Pushing down on the shutter release button opens the shutter and exposes the film.

7. Film advance lever: Before pressing the shutter release, the user pulls the film advance lever to forward the film to the next frame.

8. Hot shoe: The hot shoe holds the camera's flash.

9. Pentaprism: The pentaprism is a five-sided glass prism that is part of the camera's viewfinder system. It directs light from the lens into the viewfinder, so that a person can see the scene being photographed while focusing the camera. The picture will appear right-side up and the right way around, unlike in other types of cameras, where images appear reversed and upside down.

10. Flash: Electronic flashes provide a light source when there is not enough natural light to take a photograph. Early methods of creating a flash of light included using flash powder. Flash powder was a combination of powdered chemicals that was lit with a flint. It was highly explosive, and some photographers lost arms or legs, or even their lives, while lighting pictures with flash powder.

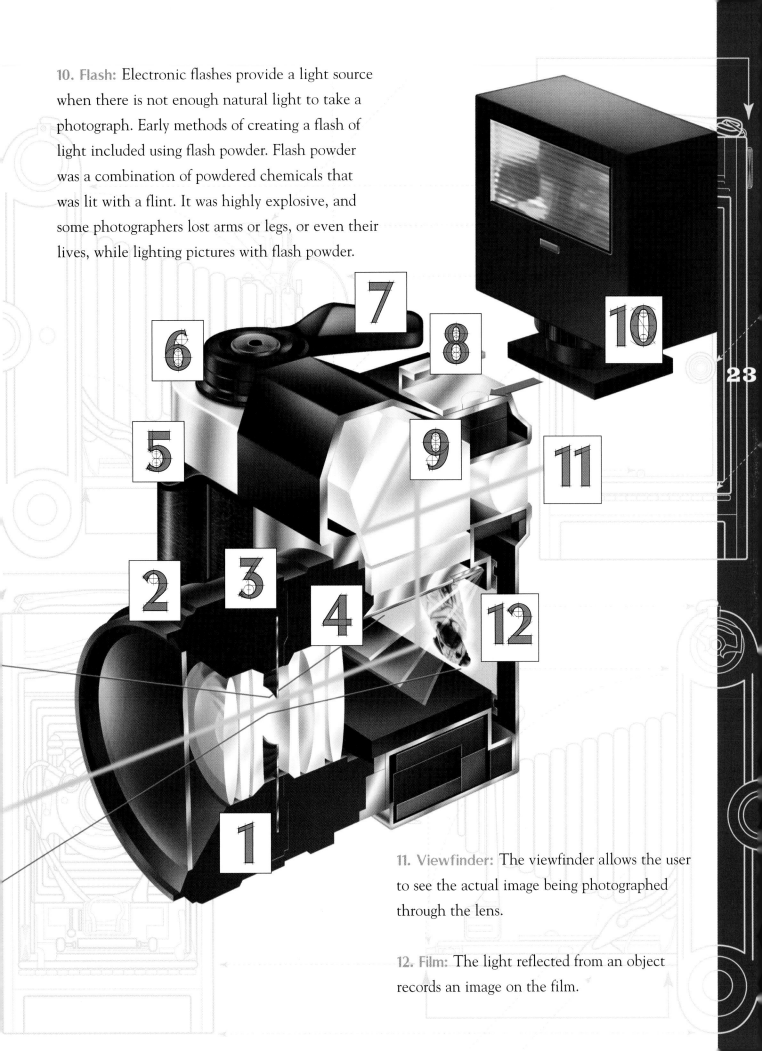

11. Viewfinder: The viewfinder allows the user to see the actual image being photographed through the lens.

12. Film: The light reflected from an object records an image on the film.

Going Digital

Digital cameras do not use film. Instead, they record images as long series of numbers that computers read and store. The numbers are known as digital information, and the process is called digital imaging.

The Filmless Camera

As computers became more common in the home in the 1980s and 1990s, camera makers began to experiment with film-less cameras. They wanted to create a camera that used a personal computer to store, or print images. The first consumer digital camera was launched in 1990 by the American company Dycam. It took black-and-white images. Four years later, Apple Computer, also based in the U.S., released a color digital camera to the general public. Digital images are made up of millions of tiny colored dots called pixels. The more pixels that a camera records, the sharper the image it produces.

(above) Digital imaging has been around since the 1960s, when the National Aeronautics and Space Administration (NASA) used computer technology to take images of planets and distant galaxies from space.

(right) Most digital cameras store images on small, removable devices, such as memory cards or disks. They can hold up to several thousand images and be reused.

Software brightens, sharpens, and enlarges digital images, changes or enhances colors, and applies special effects. The image on the right was created with image editing software.

Developing Images

Digital images are not developed in the same way as traditional photographs. On most digital cameras, a user views the picture he or she has taken on a screen on the back of the camera. Unwanted images are deleted, and the rest are transferred to a computer or printer.

People use software, either created for a computer or built into a camera or printer, to **edit** digital images. Then, they send their pictures to friends and family by e-mail, or store them on the Internet in digital "photo albums." Some people keep "photoblogs," or photo Web logs, which are online personal journals made up mostly of photographs.

Changing the Focus

With the increased popularity of digital imaging, many manufacturers are now producing digital cameras instead of or in addition to film cameras. Some manufacturers have experienced difficulty adapting to the changing industry and have laid off thousands of employees or gone out of business. Photo labs, which have traditionally processed film, have added or switched to digital services.

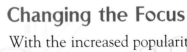

Some photo labs offer digital printing kiosks, where people print the pictures they want.

Part of Daily Life

Once cameras became common in the early 1900s, people used them to create permanent memories of events in their lives. For some people, photography became a more serious hobby. Camera clubs, specialty photography magazines, and home darkrooms all became popular.

The Camera at Work

In the 1800s, the invention of the daguerreotype led to the rise of the professional portrait photographer. Today, professional photographers also specialize in fashion, food, home and garden, travel, sports, wildlife, and celebrity photography. Their work appears in newspaper and magazine articles, advertisements, books, and calendars.

Photojournalism

Photojournalism is a form of newspaper and magazine reporting using photographs. The first news photographs were published in the *Canadian Illustrated News* in 1869. Photographs became the most common form of news illustration by the early 1900s. Today, the work of photojournalists appears not only in newspapers and magazines, but their digital images are published on Internet news sites just seconds after they are taken.

Before cameras were invented, families hired artists to paint their portraits. Today, people snap quick pictures to record important moments, such as births, graduations, weddings, and vacations.

Photography as an Art Form

Many artists have adopted photography as a way of expressing themselves creatively. Ansel Adams (1902–1984) is best known for his photographs of landscapes, while Henri Cartier-Bresson (1908–2004) is famous for his photographs of life on the streets of Paris. Yousuf Karsh (1908–2003) and Annie Leibovitz (1949–) are well known for their portraits of world leaders and celebrities.

Ansel Adams was inspired to photograph America's wilderness after visiting Yosemite Valley at the age of 14. This Adams photo shows Yosemite during a thunderstorm.

No Photos, Please

People in certain communities and cultures do not like to be photographed. Some believe that a photograph steals part of a person's soul. In Europe and North America, the most traditional Mennonite communities forbid taking photographs of people. This rule is based on a strict interpretation of a passage in the Bible, the Christian holy book, which states that people should not make images of anything in heaven, on Earth, or in the water. In the Muslim world, many women choose not to be photographed for reasons of modesty.

Specialized Cameras

O ver the past century, improvements in design and technology have led to a variety of specialized cameras. From Hollywood to the crime laboratory, the camera obscura has evolved to meet the varied needs of different users.

The Motion Picture Camera

In 1888, American inventor Thomas Edison patented the first motion picture, or movie, camera. Movie cameras work in much the same way as "still" cameras, except that they usually take many pictures each second. The human eye does not see the pictures, projected one after the other, as individual images, but as a single moving scene. Today, some movie cameras use film, while others are digital movie cameras.

Close-Up Cameras

Photography is used to document both the tiniest objects on Earth and the most immense objects in space. Scientists take pictures of highly magnified objects, such as pollen or lice, by installing special cameras into microscopes. This process is called photomicrography. Astronomers take clear photographs of objects in space with cameras built into high-powered telescopes.

A camera attached to a scanning electron microscope took these highly magnified pictures of bacteria.

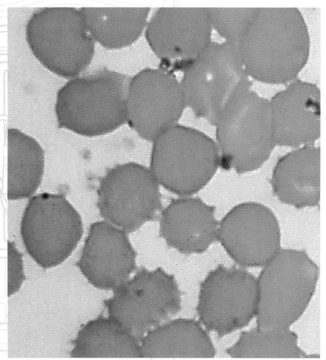
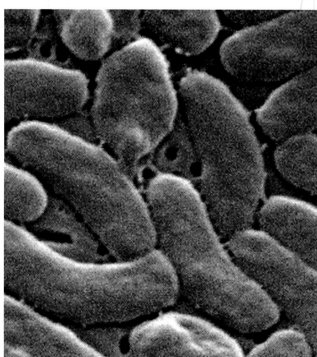

Into the Deep

Underwater cameras, which must be completely **watertight**, have allowed scuba divers and **marine biologists** to bring back images of their explorations. In 1856, an English **naturalist** named William Thompson took the first underwater photograph by placing his camera inside a watertight wooden and glass box and lowering it 18 feet (5.5 meters) beneath the sea.

Underwater camera housings improved greatly in the next hundred years. Jacques Cousteau, a French undersea explorer, helped invent the first camera with a watertight body, called the Calypso, which was first used in 1960. Today, cameras fitted into robotic submarines travel to the ocean floor, capturing images of little-known animal species and long-lost sunken ships, such as the *Titanic*.

(below) Satellite cameras take continuous pictures from space. Meteorologists use satellite images, such as this one of a hurricane approaching land, to track and predict weather patterns.

Infrared Cameras

Infrared cameras use film that is sensitive to invisible rays of light called infrared. Objects give off infrared rays in the form of heat, so infrared photographs are able to show the presence of objects even in the dark. The military uses infrared cameras for surveillance, or observing people under suspicion. The police use infrared cameras to find missing people and criminals. Crime scene analysts use them to photograph bloodstains on dark fabric.

(above) Underwater cameras allow marine biologists to photograph unusual species of coral, plants, and animals.

Cameras Tomorrow

The digital camera has changed the world of photography. People today are more likely to take pictures with digital cameras, including Web cams and camera phones, than with film cameras. Future innovations will further expand the possibilities of photography.

On the Horizon

Cameras of all types are becoming smaller, lighter, and easier to use. The quality of lenses is improving. A camera's moving parts are becoming quieter, and there is less vibration. All of this means that photos are less likely to look blurry, or out of focus.

Innovations in Digital Cameras

Many technological changes involve digital cameras. Experts predict that memory cards, which hold the digital information needed to form an image, will soon be unnecessary. Instead, images will be saved in the large built-in memories of the cameras themselves. Digital cameras with built-in satellite positioning systems will be able to detect photographers' exact locations, and automatically add this information to files on memory cards. This information could be used by police officers after evidence is photographed, as well as people in the military, surveyors, and many others.

(above) This tiny, yo-yo-like remote-controlled camera is operated by the keypad on a cell phone, or by computer. In the future, cameras such as this might be used to examine places that are too dangerous for humans to enter, such as collapsed mines and underground pipelines.

(left) In the near future, camera phones will be more popular with the general public than regular digital cameras. The increased use of wireless technology will allow users to send snapshots to home printers or picture kiosks for printing, all without wires or cables.

(below) *This digital camera is so small and light that it can be worn on a neck strap or attached to a key chain.*

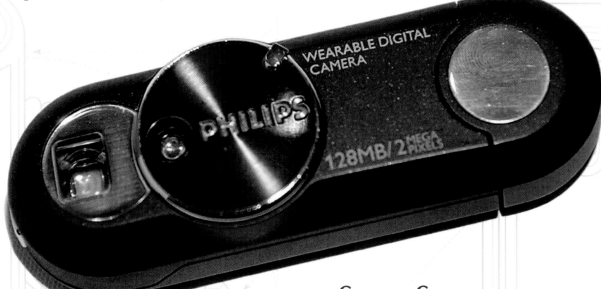

(below) *Many digital cameras use batteries that contain toxic substances, which can enter water sources, soil, and the air after they are disposed of in garbage dumps. New types of batteries, such as nickel-metal hydride and lithium ion batteries, contain materials that are less harmful to the environment.*

Camera Concerns

Cameras have benefited people in many ways, but their manufacture and use have led to a number of environmental concerns. Some chemicals used in the photographic industry can harm people and the environment. Many photo-finishing labs now reuse and recycle these chemicals rather than pour them down the drain, so they do not enter the water supply.

At home, many people print digital camera images using inkjet printers. The ink cartridges are plastic and can take 1,000 years to decompose, or break down in the soil. Today, recycling programs for these cartridges, as well as for single use, or "disposable," cameras exist. Old cartridges, and the electronics inside old cameras, are used to make new cameras.

Glossary

American Civil War A war fought in the United States between the northern and southern states from 1861 to 1865

astronomer A person who studies the stars, planets, and moons

Christian Belonging to the religion of Christianity. Christians believe in one God and follow the teachings of Jesus Christ

circuit An arrangement of electronic parts that form a path through which an electric current travels

coral A hard substance that is made by tiny marine animals called polyps

darkroom A room that no light can enter and where photographs are developed

edit To change the appearance of something, such as a photograph, to achieve a particular effect

exposure time The amount of time needed for light to shine on a plate or film so that an image appears

flexible Able to be bent without being damaged

frame An exposure, or single image, on a strip of film

Latin The language of the ancient Romans and the Roman Catholic Church

manually By hand

marine biologist A person who studies plants and animals found in seas and oceans

meteorologist A person who studies weather

modesty Proper behavior and dress

Muslim Belonging to the religion of Islam. Muslims believe in one God, called Allah, and follow the teachings of his prophets, the last of whom was Muhammad

naturalist A person who studies plants and animals

patent A legal document that prevents people from using an inventor's ideas for a certain period of time without giving the inventor proper recognition and payment

philosopher A person who tries to answer questions about truth, right and wrong, God, and the meaning of life

prototype The first full-size, usually working model of an invention

scholar A well educated person

solar eclipse Occurs when the Moon passes between the Sun and the Earth, blocking the Sun's light

solution A mixture made by dissolving substances in a liquid

starch A tasteless, white carbohydrate found in foods such as potatoes and rice

tarnish To become discolored, especially by exposure to air

transparent Allowing light to pass through so that something behind can be seen

watertight Sealed so water does not enter

Web cam A camera that takes a digital video and transmits it over the Internet

World War I A war fought by countries around the world from 1914 to 1918

Index

1 2 3 4 5 6 7 8 9 0   Printed in the U.S.A.   5 4 3 2 1 0 9 8 7 6